THE WRITER'S QUOTATION BOOK

The Writer's Quotation Book

A literary companion

PUSHCART

EDITED BY JAMES CHARLTON

SECOND PRINTING SEPTEMBER 1980

Library of Congress Card Number: 79-88700
ISBN: 0-916366-08-1

MANUFACTURED IN THE UNITED STATES OF AMERICA

PREFACE

Writers love quotations. They love quoting someone else's work almost as much as they enjoy quoting their own. We consider a well-placed quotation in a conversation, whether it be Shakespeare, Cervantes or Groucho Marx, to be one of the marks of an erudite and educated individual. And it lends weight to one's own opinions by somehow invoking a higher authority.

I had been collecting favorite quotations about writing and books for years, scraps of paper, news clippings, almost anything with well-polished and cleverly turned phrases on them. Writing and editing—two occupations which have more or less paid my rent over a number of years—can be whimsical, frustrating and lonely, and many of the quotations reflect those qualities.

Recently the company for which I am editor-in-chief needed some sort of giveaway for the national booksellers' meeting, the annual three-ring circus where publishing houses display their wares. I suggested a short collection of quotations made up mostly of what I had in the drawer. To add to those I asked a number of friends and acquaintances to send me their favorites. What I thought was a solitary indulgence turned out to be a pastime practiced by a number of people involved with books. Aphorisms, witticisms, bons mots, palindromes, gossip, poems, metaphors from the present and past centuries poured in as soon as I asked people to share their favorite literary clipping or sampler with me.

The result was a small handout that not only competed with tote bags, T-shirts, buttons and the occasional book at the ABA convention, but also was mentioned in newspapers across the country. A number of requests for the collection came in from readers around the world and, unexpectedly, a great many additional quotations came in as well. Best of all, Bill Henderson, publisher of the prestigious Pushcart Press, offered to publish a book if I would greatly expand the collection of quotations. I was delighted to oblige.

Many people contributed to making this collection the enjoyable effort that it was, and I would like to thank them. "To be amused by what you read—that is the great spring of happy quotations," penned C. E. Montague in A Writer's Notes to His Trade, and I think all writers, readers and their friends will find this book amusing, entertaining and instructive.

JAMES CHARLTON
New York

THE WRITER'S QUOTATION BOOK

The last thing that we find in making a book is to know what we must put first.

BLAISE PASCAL

There is nothing so important as the book can be.

MAXWELL PERKINS

It is a great thing to start life with a small number of really good books which are your very own.

SHERLOCK HOLMES

The walls of books around him, dense with the past, formed a kind of insulation against the present world and its disasters.

ROSS MACDONALD

An ordinary man can . . . surround himself with two thousand books . . . and thenceforward have at least one place in the world in which it is possible to be happy.

AUGUSTINE BIRRELL

Only one hour in the normal day is more pleasurable than the hour spent in bed with a book before going to sleep, and that is the hour spent in bed with a book after being called in the morning.

ROSE MACAULAY

The pleasure of all reading is doubled when one lives with another who shares the same books.

KATHERINE MANSFIELD

Talk of the happiness of getting a great prize in the lottery! What is that to the opening of a box of books! The joy upon lifting up the cover must be something like what we feel when Peter the Porter opens the door upstairs, and says, "Please to walk in, sir."

ROBERT SOUTHEY

Just the knowledge that a good book is waiting one at the end of a long day makes that day happier.

KATHLEEN NORRIS

Books are a delightful society. If you go into a room filled with books, even without taking them down from their shelves, they seem to speak to you, to welcome you.

WILLIAM E. GLADSTONE

There are books which I love to see on the shelf. I feel a virtue goes out of them, but I should think it undue familiarity to read them.

SAMUEL MCCHORD CROTHERS

Americans like fat books and thin women.

RUSSELL BAKER

In a very real sense, people who have read good literature have lived more than people who cannot or will not read. . . . It is not true that we have only one life to live; if we can read, we can live as many more lives and as many kinds of lives as we wish.

S. I. HAYAKAWA

This will never be a civilized country until we expend more money for books than we do for chewing gum.

ELBERT HUBBARD

The man who does not read good books has no advantage over the man who can't read them.

MARK TWAIN

Books are fatal: they are the curse of the human race. Nine-tenths of existing books are nonsense, and the clever books are the refutation of that nonsense. The greatest misfortune that ever befell man was the invention of printing.

BENJAMIN DISRAELI

In literature, as in love, we are astonished at what is chosen by others.

ANDRÉ MAUROIS

Sir, the fact that a book is in the public library brings no comfort. Books are the one element in which I am personally and nakedly acquisitive. If it weren't for the law I would steal them. If it weren't for my purse I would buy them.

HAROLD LASKI

Never lend books, for no one ever returns them; the only books I have in my library are books that other folk have lent me.

ANATOLE FRANCE

When I get a little money, I buy books; and if any is left, I buy food and clothes.
DESIDERIUS ERASMUS

Hard-covered books break up friendships. You loan a hard-covered book to a friend and when he doesn't return it you get mad at him. It makes you mean and petty. But twenty-five cent books are different.
JOHN STEINBECK

The multitude of books is making us ignorant.
VOLTAIRE

There are times when I think that the reading I have done in the past has had no effect except to cloud my mind and make me indecisive.
ROBERTSON DAVIES

If we encounter a man of rare intellect, we should ask him what books he reads.
RALPH WALDO EMERSON

If I read a book that impresses me, I have to take myself firmly in hand before I mix with other people; otherwise they would think my mind rather queer.
ANNE FRANK

A book is a mirror; if an ass peers into it, you can't expect an apostle to peer out.
GEORG CHRISTOPH LICHTENBERG

We live in an age that reads too much to be wise.
OSCAR WILDE

The best effect of any book is that it excites the reader to self-activity.
THOMAS CARLYLE

A man may as well expect to grow stronger by always eating as wiser by always reading.
JEREMY COLLIER

Reading is to the mind what exercise is to the body.
SIR RICHARD STEELE

A book is like a garden carried in the pocket.
CHINESE PROVERB

These are not books, lumps of lifeless paper, but *minds* alive on the shelves. From each of them goes out its own voice . . . and just as the touch of a button on our set will fill the room with music, so by taking down one of these volumes and opening it, one can call into range the voice of a man far distant in time and space, and hear him speaking to us, mind to mind, heart to heart.
GILBERT HIGHET

There is more treasure in books than in all the pirates' loot on Treasure Island . . . and best of all, you can enjoy these riches every day of your life.
WALT DISNEY

I would never read a book if it were possible for me
to talk half an hour with the man who wrote it.

WOODROW WILSON

Child! Do not throw this book about;
Refrain from the unholy pleasure of cutting
all the pictures out!
Preserve it as your chiefest treasure.

HILAIRE BELLOC

No woman was ever ruined by a book.

MAYOR JIMMY WALKER *of New York City*

Those whom books will hurt will not be proof against
events. If some books are deemed more baneful and their
sale forbid, how, then, with deadlier facts, not dreams of
doting men? Events, not books, should be forbid.

HERMAN MELVILLE

There is a great deal of difference between an eager man
who wants to read a book and a tired man who wants
a book to read.

G. K. CHESTERTON

Many persons read and like fiction. It does not tax the
intelligence and the intelligence of most of us can so
ill afford taxation that we rightly welcome any reading
matter which avoids this.

ROSE MACAULAY

I divide all readers into two classes; those who read to remember and those who read to forget.

WILLIAM LYON PHELPS

As a rule reading fiction is as hard to me as trying to hit a target by hurling feathers at it. I need *resistance* to cerebrate!

WILLIAM JAMES

No man understands a deep book until he has seen and lived at least part of its contents.

EZRA POUND

When you reread a classic you do not see more in the book than you did before; you see more in *you* than was there before.

CLIFTON FADIMAN

The art of reading is in great part that of acquiring a better understanding of life from one's encounter with it in a book.

ANDRÉ MAUROIS

There are some books one needs maturity to enjoy just as there are books an adult can come upon too late to savor.

PHYLLIS MCGINLEY

The road to ignorance is paved with good editions.

GEORGE BERNARD SHAW

Every man who knows how to read has it in his power to magnify himself, to multiply the ways in which he exists, to make his life full, significant and interesting.

ALDOUS HUXLEY

I suggest that the only books that influence us are those for which we are ready, and which have gone a little farther down our particular path than we have yet gone ourselves.

E. M. FORSTER

When we read too fast or too slowly, we understand nothing.

BLAISE PASCAL

Who knows if Shakespeare might not have thought less if he had read more.

EDWARD YOUNG

The players often mention it as an honor to Shakespeare that in his writing, whatsoever he penned, he never blotted out a line. My answer hath been, "Would he had blotted a thousand."

BEN JONSON

I have not wasted my life trifling with literary fools in taverns as Jonson did when he should have been shaking England with the thunder of his spirit.

GEORGE BERNARD SHAW

Where is human nature so weak as in the bookstore?
HENRY WARD BEECHER

The oldest books are still only just out to those who
have not read them.
SAMUEL BUTLER

The worst thing about new books is that they keep us
from reading the old ones.
JOSEPH JOUBERT

There is a good saying to the effect that when a new
book appears one should read an old one. As an author
I would not recommend too strict an adherence to this
saying.
WINSTON CHURCHILL

The public which reads, in any sense of the word worth
considering, is very, very small; the public which would
feel no lack if all book-printing ceased tomorrow is
enormous.
GEORGE GISSING

Of course no writers ever forget their first acceptance.
. . . One fine day when I was seventeen I had my first,
second and third, all in the same morning's mail. Oh,
I'm here to tell you, dizzy with excitement is no mere
phrase!
TRUMAN CAPOTE

Publication—is the auction of the Mind of Man.

EMILY DICKINSON

One old lady who wants her head lifted wouldn't be so bad, but you multiply her two hundred and fifty thousand times and what you get is a book club.

FLANNERY O'CONNOR

For several days after my first book was published I carried it about in my pocket, and took surreptitious peeps at it to make sure the ink had not faded.

SIR JAMES M. BARRIE

On the day when a young writer corrects his first proof-sheet he is as proud as a schoolboy who has just gotten his first dose of the pox.

CHARLES BAUDELAIRE

Most of the basic material a writer works with is acquired before the age of fifteen.

WILLA CATHER

For a dyed-in-the-wool author nothing is as dead as a book once it is written. . . . She is rather like a cat whose kittens have grown-up. While they were a-growing she was passionately interested in them but now they seem hardly to belong to her—and probably she is involved with another batch of kittens as I am involved with other writing.

RUMER GODDEN

I am very foolish over my own book. I have a copy which I constantly read and find very illuminating. Swift confesses to something of the sort with his own compositions.

J. B. YEATS *in a letter to his son,* W. B. YEATS

I don't keep any copy of my books around. . . . They would embarrass me. When I finish writing my books, I kick them in the belly, and have done with them.

LUDWIG BEMELMANS

As for my next book, I am going to hold myself from writing it till I have it impending in me: grown heavy in my mind like a ripe pear; pendant, gravid, asking to be cut or it will fall.

VIRGINIA WOOLF

Looking back, I imagine I was always writing. Twaddle it was too. But better far write twaddle or anything, anything, than nothing at all.

KATHERINE MANSFIELD

I suppose I am a born novelist, for the things I imagine are more vital and vivid to me than the things I remember.

ELLEN GLASGOW

If we should ever inaugurate a hall of fame, it would be reserved exclusively and hopefully for authors who, having written four bestsellers, *still refrained* from starting out on a lecture tour.

E. B. WHITE

Almost all the great writers have as their *motif*, more or less disguised, the "passage from childhood to maturity," the clash between the thrill of expectation, and the disillusioning knowledge of the truth. *Lost Illusion* is the undisclosed title of every novel.

ANDRÉ MAUROIS

"Was it Eliot's toilet I saw?"
Palindrome allegedly uttered by an American publisher after paying his first visit to the London firm of Faber and Faber

In order to predict the popularity of a particular book, specially designed tests can be made on potential readers with excerpts from that book. By submitting a manuscript to a scientifically selected panel of people, with the proper techniques for recording their reactions, a forecast of the probable success of a book can be made.

HENRY LINK *and* HARRY HOPF, *from* People and Books: A Study of Reading and Bookbuying Habits, *issued in 1946*

There are some books of which scores of copies are bought for one which is read, and others which have dozens of readers for every copy sold.

JOHN AYSCOUGH

What a sense of superiority it gives one to escape reading a book which everyone else is reading.

ALICE JAMES

There are two motives for reading a book; one, that you enjoy it; the other, that you can boast about it.
BERTRAND RUSSELL

What can I tell the buyers? I often think how shocked authors would be if they listened to the salesmen selling their books. They've worked a year on their book—two years, three years, maybe longer. And there it is. A word or two and a decision is made.
BRUCE BLIVEN, *quoting book salesman George Scheer*

Best-Sellerism is the star system of the book world. A "best-seller" is a celebrity among books. It is known primarily (sometimes exclusively) for its well-knownness.
DANIEL J. BOORSTIN

A best-seller is the gilded tomb of a mediocre talent.
LOGAN PEARSALL SMITH

The secret of popular writing is never to put more on a given page than the common reader can lap off it with no strain WHATSOEVER on his habitually slack attention.
EZRA POUND

It circulated for five years, through the halls of fifteen publishers, and finally ended up with Vanguard Press, which, as you can see, is rather deep into the alphabet.
PATRICK DENNIS *commenting on* Auntie Mame

When one says that a writer is fashionable one practically always means that he is admired by people under thirty.

GEORGE ORWELL

I couldn't write the things they publish now, with no beginning and no end, and a little incest in the middle.

IRVIN S. COBB

In America only the successful writer is important, in France all writers are important, in England no writer is important, in Australia you have to explain what a writer is.

GEOFFREY COTTERELL

Literature plays an important role in our country, helping the Party to educate the people correctly, to instill in them advanced, progressive ideas by which our Party is guided. And it is not without reason that writers in our country are called engineers of the human soul.

NIKITA KHRUSHCHEV

No wonder the really powerful men in our society, whether politicians or scientists, hold writers and poets in contempt. They do it because they get no evidence from modern literature that anybody is thinking about any significant question.

SAUL BELLOW

Sir, no man but a blockhead ever wrote except for money.

SAMUEL JOHNSON

America is about the last place in which life will be endurable at all for an inspired writer.

SAMUEL BUTLER

Instead of marvelling with Johnson, how anything but profit should incite men to literary labour, I am rather surprised that mere emolument should induce them to labour so well.

THOMAS GREEN

Almost anyone can be an author; the business is to collect money and fame from this state of being.

A. A. MILNE

Writing is the only profession where no one considers you ridiculous if you earn no money.

JULES RENARD

Years ago, to say you were a writer was not the highest recommendation to your landlord. Today, he at least hesitates before he refuses to rent you an apartment—for all he knows you may be rich.

ARTHUR MILLER

The profession of book-writing makes horse racing seem like a solid, stable business.

JOHN STEINBECK

Anything that is written to please the author is worthless.

BLAISE PASCAL

If writers were good businessmen, they'd have too much sense to be writers.

IRVIN S. COBB

The multitude of books is a great evil. There is no measure or limit to this fever of writing; everyone must be an author, some for some kind of vanity to acquire celebrity and raise a name, others for the sake of lucre or gain.

MARTIN LUTHER

I do think that the quality which makes a man want to write and be read is essentially a desire for self-exposure and is masochistic. Like one of those guys who has a compulsion to take his thing out and show it on the street.

JAMES JONES

A man really writes for an audience of about ten persons. Of course, if others like it, that is clear gain. But if those ten are satisfied, he is content.

ALFRED NORTH WHITEHEAD

I write what I would like to read—what I think other women would like to read. If what I write makes a woman in the Canadian mountains cry and she writes and tells me about it, especially if she says, "I read it to Tom when he came in from work and he cried too," I feel I have succeeded.

KATHLEEN NORRIS, *on the publication of her seventy-eighth book*

My purpose is to entertain myself first and other people secondly.

JOHN D. MACDONALD

When I write, I aim in my mind not toward New York but toward a vague spot a little east of Kansas. I think of the books on library shelves, without their jackets, years old, and a countryish teen-aged boy finding them, and having them speak to him. The reviews, the stacks in Brentano's, are just hurdles to get over, to place the books on that shelf.

JOHN UPDIKE

Writing is one of the few professions left where you take all the responsibility for what you do. It's really dangerous and ultimately destroys you as a writer if you start thinking about responses to your work or what your audience needs.

ERICA JONG

Writers, if they are worthy of that jealous designation, do not write for other writers. They write to give reality to experience.

ARCHIBALD MACLEISH

In a very real sense, the writer writes in order to teach himself, to understand himself, to satisfy himself; the publishing of his ideas, though it brings gratifications, is a curious anticlimax.

ALFRED KAZIN

Any writer overwhelmingly honest about pleasing himself is almost sure to please others.
MARIANNE MOORE

Success comes to a writer, as a rule, so gradually that it is always something of a shock to him to look back and realize the heights to which he has climbed.
P. G. WODEHOUSE

Word has somehow got around that the split infinitive is always wrong. That is a piece with the outworn notion that it is always wrong to strike a lady.
JAMES THURBER

I often think how much easier life would have been for me and how much time I would have saved if I had known the alphabet. I can never tell where *I* and *J* stand without saying *G, H* to myself first. I don't know whether *P* comes before *R* or after, and where *T* comes in has to this day remained something that I have never been able to get into my head.
W. SOMERSET MAUGHAM

Any writer worth the name is always getting into one thing or getting out of another thing.
FANNIE HURST

Writing is easy; all you do is sit staring at a blank sheet of paper until the drops of blood form on your forehead.
GENE FOWLER

When I stepped from hard manual work to writing, I just stepped from one kind of hard work to another.
SEAN O'CASEY

In stating as fully as I could how things really were, it was often very difficult and I wrote awkwardly and the awkwardness is what they called my style. All mistakes and awkwardness are easy to see, and they called it style.
ERNEST HEMINGWAY

Nothing you write, if you hope to be any good, will ever come out as you first hoped.
LILLIAN HELLMAN

I have rewritten—often several times—every word I have ever published. My pencils outlast their erasures.
VLADIMIR NABOKOV

Read over your compositions and, when you meet a passage which you think is particularly fine, strike it out.
SAMUEL JOHNSON

I'm a lousy writer; a helluva lot of people have got lousy taste.
GRACE METALIOUS

Those big-shot writers . . . could never dig the fact that there are more salted peanuts consumed than caviar.
MICKEY SPILLANE

To write simply is as difficult as to be good.
W. SOMERSET MAUGHAM

A bad book is as much a labor to write as a good one;
it comes as sincerely from the author's soul.
ALDOUS HUXLEY

It takes less time to learn to write nobly than to learn to
write lightly and straightforwardly.
FRIEDRICH WILHELM NIETZSCHE

All a writer has to do is get a woman to say he's a writer;
it's an aphrodisiac.
SAUL BELLOW

Pretty women swarm around everybody but writers. Plain,
intelligent women *somewhat*, swarm around writers.
WILLIAM SAROYAN

The sinister thing about writing is that it starts off seeming
so easy and ends up being so hard. . . . As an editor over
many years, I met hundreds of writers, and I don't think
I ever met one for whom writing wasn't a misery. But
writing does not *cause* misery, it is born of misery, as
Montaigne said.
L. RUST HILLS

Most writers are in a state of gloom a good deal of the
time; they need perpetual reassurance.
JOHN HALL WHEELOCK

I love being a writer. What I can't stand is the paperwork.

PETER DE VRIES

Read, read, read. Read everything—trash, classics, good and bad, and see how they do it. Just like a carpenter who works as an apprentice and studies the master. Read! You'll absorb it. Then write. If it is good, you'll find out. If it's not, throw it out the window.

WILLIAM FAULKNER

Writing is not a profession but a vocation of unhappiness.

GEORGES SIMENON

I am convinced that all writers are optimists whether they concede the point or not. . . . How otherwise could any human being sit down to a pile of blank sheets and decide to write, say two hundred thousand words on a given theme?

THOMAS COSTAIN

Whatever our theme in writing, it is old and tried. Whatever our place, it has been visited by the stranger, it will never be new again. It is only the vision that can be new; but that is enough.

EUDORA WELTY

The writer, like the priest, must be exempted from secular labor. His work needs a frolic health; he must be at the top of his condition.

RALPH WALDO EMERSON

The writer has taken unto himself the former function of the priest or prophet. He presumes to order and legislate the people's life. There is no person more arrogant than the writer.

CORNELIUS REGISTER

What release to write so that one forgets oneself, forgets one's companion, forgets where one is or what one is going to do next—to be drenched in sleep or in the sea. Pencils and pads and curling blue sheets alive with letters heap up on the desk.

ANNE MORROW LINDBERGH

Another damned thick, square book! Always scribble, scribble! Eh! Mr. Gibbon?

THE DUKE OF GLOUCESTER, *upon accepting the second volume of* A History of the Decline and Fall of the Roman Empire *from its author*

The devoted writer of humor must continue to try to come as close to the truth as he can, even if he gets burned in the process, but I don't think he will get too badly burned. His faith in the good will, the soundness, and the sense of humor of his countrymen will always serve as his asbestos curtain.

JAMES THURBER

A well-written life is almost as rare as a well-spent one.

THOMAS CARLYLE

It took me fifteen years to discover I had no talent for writing, but I couldn't give it up because by that time I was too famous.

ROBERT BENCHLEY

You must not suppose, because I am a man of letters, that I never tried to earn an honest living.

GEORGE BERNARD SHAW

I wrote a short story because I wanted to see something of mine in print other than my fingers.

WILSON MIZNER

Boozing does not necessarily have to go hand in hand with being a writer, as seems to be the concept in America. I therefore solemnly declare to all young men trying to become writers that they do not actually have to become drunkards first.

NELSON W. ALDRICH

Some American writers who have known each other for years have never met in the daytime or when both were sober.

JAMES THURBER

It is the part of prudence to thank an author for his book before reading it, so as to avoid the necessity of lying about it afterwards.

GEORGE SANTAYANA

I put a piece of paper under my pillow, and when I could not sleep I wrote in the dark.

HENRY DAVID THOREAU

Failure is very difficult for a writer to bear, but very few can manage the shock of early success.

MAURICE VALENCY

This is what I find most encouraging about the writing trades: They allow mediocre people who are patient and industrious to revise their stupidity, to edit themselves into something like intelligence. They also allow lunatics to seem saner than sane.

KURT VONNEGUT, JR.

Some men borrow books; some men steal books; and others beg presentation copies from the author.

JAMES JEFFREY ROCHE

From the moment I picked your book up until I laid it down I was convulsed with laughter. Someday I intend reading it.

GROUCHO MARX, *on S. J. Perelman's first book*

Writing is a solitary occupation. Family, friends, and society are the natural enemies of a writer. He must be alone, uninterrupted, and slightly savage if he is to sustain and complete an undertaking.

LAWRENCE CLARK POWELL

He has left off reading altogether, to the great improvement of his originality.

EDWARD YOUNG

No one can write decently who is distrustful of the reader's intelligence, or whose attitude is patronizing.

E. B. WHITE

If you want to get rich from writing, write the sort of thing that's read by persons who move their lips when they're reading to themselves.

DON MARQUIS

The most essential gift for a good writer is a built-in shock-proof shit-detector.

ERNEST HEMINGWAY

Nature, not content with denying him the ability to think, has endowed him with the ability to write.

A. E. HOUSMAN

It is a fact that few novelists enjoy the creative labour, though most enjoy thinking about the creative labour.

ARNOLD BENNETT

Everything goes by the board: honor, pride, decency . . . to get the book written. If a writer has to rob his mother, he will not hesitate; the *Ode on a Grecian Urn* is worth any number of old ladies.

WILLIAM FAULKNER

Writing is an adventure. To begin with, it is a toy and an amusement. Then it becomes a mistress, then it becomes a master, then it becomes a tyrant. The last phase is that just as you are about to be reconciled to your servitude, you kill the monster and fling him to the public.

WINSTON CHURCHILL

Literature is an occupation in which you have to keep proving your talent to people who have none.

JULES RENARD

The difference between journalism and literature is that journalism is unreadable and literature is not read.

OSCAR WILDE

When a book, any sort of book, reaches a certain intensity of artistic performance it becomes literature. That intensity may be a matter of style, situation, character, emotional tone, or idea, or half a dozen other things. It may also be a perfection of control over the movement of a story similar to the control a great pitcher has over a ball.

RAYMOND CHANDLER

Poets are like baseball pitchers. Both have their moments. The intervals are the tough things.

ROBERT FROST

They can't yank a novelist like they can a pitcher. A novelist has to go the full nine, even if it kills him.

ERNEST HEMINGWAY

There's nothing to writing. All you do is sit down at a typewriter and open a vein.

RED SMITH

Sometimes I think it sounds like I walked out of the room and left the typewriter running.

GENE FOWLER

The machine has several virtues. . . . One may lean back in his chair and work it. It piles an awful stack of words on one page. It don't muss things or scatter ink blots around.

from MARK TWAIN'S *first letter written on a typewriter*

We romantic writers are there to make people feel and not think. A historical romance is the only kind of book where chastity really counts.

BARBARA CARTLAND

People do not deserve to have good writing, they are so pleased with bad.

RALPH WALDO EMERSON

I think you must remember that a writer is a simple-minded person to begin with and go on that basis. He's not a great mind, he's not a great thinker, he's not a great philosopher, he's a storyteller.

ERSKINE CALDWELL

Immature artists imitate. Mature artists steal.
LIONEL TRILLING

Remember why the good Lord made your eyes
Pla-gi-a-rize!
TOM LEHRER

Next o'er his books his eyes began to roll,
In pleasing memory of all he stole.
ALEXANDER POPE

Just get it down on paper, and then we'll see what to do
with it.
MAXWELL PERKINS'S *advice to Marcia Davenport*

Never make excuses, never let them see you bleed, and
never get separated from your baggage.
from WESLEY PRICE'S *"Three Rules of Professional Comportment for Writers"*

The tools I need for my work are paper, tobacco, food,
and a little whisky.
WILLIAM FAULKNER

The ideal view for daily writing, hour on hour, is the
blank brick wall of a cold-storage warehouse. Failing
this, a stretch of sky will do, cloudless if possible.
EDNA FERBER

The perfect place for a writer is in the hideous roar of a city, with men making a new road under his window in competition with a barrel organ, and on the mat a man waiting for the rent.

HENRY VOLLAM MORTON

The best time for planning a book is while you're doing the dishes.

AGATHA CHRISTIE

What no wife of a writer can ever understand is that a writer is working when he's staring out of the window.

BURTON RASCOE

If I could I would always work in silence and obscurity, and let my efforts be known by their results.

EMILY BRONTË

All my major works have been written in prison. . . . I would recommend prison not only to aspiring writers but to aspiring politicians, too.

JAWAHARLAL NEHRU

Often while reading a book one feels that the author would have preferred to paint rather than write; one can sense the pleasure he derives from describing a landscape or a person, as if he were painting what he is saying, because deep in his heart he would have preferred to use brushes and colors.

PABLO PICASSO

The man of letters loves not only to be read but to be seen. Happy to be by himself, he would be happier still if people knew that he was happy to be by himself, working in solitude at night under his lamp.

REMY DE GOURMONT

Only ambitious nonentities and hearty mediocrities exhibit their rough drafts. It is like passing around samples of one's sputum.

VLADIMIR NABOKOV

I just think it's bad to talk about one's present work, for it spoils something at the root of the creative act. It discharges the tension.

NORMAN MAILER

Mostly, we authors must repeat ourselves—that's the truth. We have two or three great moving experiences in our lives—experiences so great and moving that it doesn't seem at the time that anyone else has been caught up and pounded and dazzled and astonished and beaten and broken and rescued and illuminated and rewarded and humbled in just that way ever before.

F. SCOTT FITZGERALD

I've always believed in writing without a collaborator, because where two people are writing the same book, each believes he gets all the worries and only half the royalties.

AGATHA CHRISTIE

I never could understand how two men can write a book together; to me that's like three people getting together to have a baby.

EVELYN WAUGH

Why do people always expect authors to answer questions? I am an author because I want to *ask* questions. If I had answers I'd be a politician.

EUGENE IONESCO

INTERVIEWER: *How many drafts of a story do you do?*
S. J. PERELMAN: Thirty-seven. I once tried doing thirty-three, but something was lacking, a certain—how shall I say?—*je ne sais quoi.* On another occasion, I tried forty-two versions, but the final effect was too lapidary—you know what I mean, Jack? What the hell are you trying to extort—my trade secrets?

People who read me seem to be divided into four groups: twenty-five percent like me for the right reasons; twenty-five percent like me for the wrong reasons; twenty-five percent hate me for the wrong reasons; twenty-five percent hate me for the right reasons. It's that last twenty-five percent that worries me.

ROBERT FROST

I wrote the scenes . . . by using the same apprehensive imagination that occurs in the morning before an afternoon's appointment with my dentist.

JOHN MARQUAND

An author ought to write for the youth of his own generation, the critics of the next, and the schoolmasters of ever afterwards.

F. SCOTT FITZGERALD

When I want to read a good book, I write one.

BENJAMIN DISRAELI

I never desire to converse with a man who has written more than he has read.

SAMUEL JOHNSON

Only when one has lost all curiosity about the future has one reached the age to write an autobiography.

EVELYN WAUGH

And because I found I had nothing else to write about, I presented myself as a subject.

MONTAIGNE

The man who writes about himself and his own time is the only man who writes about all people and about all time.

GEORGE BERNARD SHAW

I'll be eighty this month. Age, if nothing else, entitles me to set the record straight before I dissolve. I've given my memoirs far more thought than any of my marriages. You can't divorce a book.

GLORIA SWANSON

Just as there is nothing between the admirable omelette and the intolerable, so with autobiography.
HILAIRE BELLOC

On the trail of another man, the biographer must put up with finding himself at every turn: any biography uneasily shelters an autobiography within it.
PAUL MURRAY KENDALL

What makes a good writer of history is a guy who is suspicious. Suspicion marks the real difference between the man who wants to write honest history and the one who'd rather write a good story.
JIM BISHOP

The novel is the highest example of subtle interrelatedness that man has discovered.
D. H. LAWRENCE

Every author really wants to have letters printed in the papers. Unable to make the grade, he drops down a rung of the ladder and writes novels.
P. G. WODEHOUSE

I have never met an author who admitted that people did not buy his book because it was dull.
W. SOMERSET MAUGHAM

Writing is a dog's life, but the only life worth living.
GUSTAVE FLAUBERT

Prose books are the show dogs I breed and sell to support my cat.

ROBERT GRAVES, *on writing novels to support his love of writing poetry*

When audiences come to see us authors lecture, it is largely in the hope that we'll be funnier to look at than to read.

SINCLAIR LEWIS

A writer's problem does not change. He himself changes and the world he lives in changes, but his problem remains the same. It is always how to write truly and, having found out what is true, to project it in such a way that it becomes a part of the experience of the person who reads it.

ERNEST HEMINGWAY

Writers seldom choose as friends those self-contained characters who are never in trouble, never unhappy or ill, never make mistakes, and always count their change when it is handed to them.

CATHERINE DRINKER BOWEN

There is only one trait that marks the writer. He is always watching. It's a kind of trick of the mind and he is born with it.

MORLEY CALLAGHAN

When you're a writer, you no longer see things with the freshness of the normal person. There are always two figures that work inside you, and if you are at all intelligent you realize that you have lost something. But I think there has always been this dichotomy in a real writer. He wants to be terribly human, and he responds emotionally, and at the same time there's this cold observer who cannot cry.

BRIAN MOORE

How can you write if you can't cry?

RING LARDNER

In any work that is truly creative, I believe, the writer cannot be omniscient in advance about the effects that he proposes to produce. The suspense of a novel is not only in the reader, but in the novelist, who is intensely curious about what will happen to the hero.

MARY MCCARTHY

I can always find plenty of women to sleep with but the kind of woman that is really hard for me to find is a typist who can read my writing.

THOMAS WOLFE

They're fancy talkers about themselves, writers. If I had to give young writers advice, I would say don't listen to writers talk about writing or themselves.

LILLIAN HELLMAN

Most writers, you know, are awful sticks to talk with.

SHERWOOD ANDERSON

If I didn't know the ending of a story, I wouldn't begin. I always write my last line, my last paragraphs, my last page first.

KATHERINE ANNE PORTER

Writing every book is like a purge; at the end of it one is empty . . . like a dry shell on the beach, waiting for the tide to come in again.

DAPHNE DU MAURIER

A collection of short stories is generally thought to be a horrendous clinker; an enforced courtesy for the elderly writer who wants to display the trophies of his youth, along with his trout flies.

JOHN CHEEVER

If you are getting the worst of it in an argument with a literary man, always attack his style. That'll touch him if nothing else will.

J. A. SPENDER

Your manuscript is both good and original; but the part that is good is not original, and the part that is original is not good.

SAMUEL JOHNSON

Whenever you feel an impulse to perpetrate a piece of exceptionally fine writing, obey it . . . and delete it before sending your manuscript to the press.

SIR ARTHUR QUILLER-COUCH

Literary success of any enduring kind is made by refusing to do what publishers want, by refusing to write what the public wants, by refusing to accept any popular standard, by refusing to write anything to order.

LAFCADIO HEARN

Never submit an idea or chapter to an editor or publisher, no matter how much he would like you to. Writing from the approved idea is (another) gravely serious time-waster. This is your story. Try and find out what your editor wants in advance, but then try and give it to him in one piece.

JOHN CREASEY

Nine out of ten writers, I am sure, could write more. I think they should and, if they did, they would find their work improving even beyond their own, their agent's, and their editor's highest hopes.

JOHN CREASEY

I've never signed a contract, so never have a deadline. A deadline's an unnerving thing. I just finish a book, and if the publisher doesn't like it that's his privilege. There've been many, many rejections. If you want to write it your own way, that's the chance you take.

MARCHETTE CHUTE

The textbook companies, and beyond them the school boards, simply do not permit authors the freedom to write their own books in their own way. Today, texts are written backward or inside out, as it were, beginning with public demand and ending with the historian. This system gives the publishers a certain security, since their books cannot be too far out of the mainstream. But, having minimized one kind of risk, they have created another, of a different order.

FRANCES FITZGERALD

A book must be done according to the writer's conception of it as nearly perfect as possible, and the publishing problems begin then. That is, the publisher must not try to get a writer to fit the book to the conditions of the trade, etc. It must be the other way around.

MAXWELL PERKINS

Only a small minority of authors over-write themselves. Most of the good and the tolerable ones do not write enough.

ARNOLD BENNETT

With sixty staring me in the face, I have developed inflammation of the sentence structure and a definite hardening of the paragraphs.

JAMES THURBER, *at age 59*

In the march up the heights of fame there comes a spot close to the summit in which man reads nothing but detective stories.

HEYWOOD HALE BROUN

At least half the mystery novels published violate the law that the solution, once revealed, must seem to be inevitable.

RAYMOND CHANDLER

The beginner who submits a detective novel longer than 80,000 words is courting rejection.

HOWARD HAYCRAFT

The detective himself should never turn out to be the culprit.

S. S. VAN DINE

Love interest nearly always weakens a mystery because it introduces a type of suspense that is antagonistic to the detective's struggle to solve a problem.

RAYMOND CHANDLER

The mystery story is two stories in one: the story of what happened and the story of what appeared to happen.

MARY ROBERTS RINEHART

There certainly does seem a possibility that the detective story will come to an end, simply because the public will have learnt all the tricks.

DOROTHY SAYERS

A good science fiction story is a story with a human problem, and a human solution, which would not have happened without its science content.

THEODORE STURGEON

Science fiction is distinguished from the other genres of the fantastic by the special kind of plausibility it introduces. This plausibility is in direct proportion to the solid scientific elements the author introduces. If they fail, science fiction becomes a dead form, a stereotype.

MICHEL BUTOR

I love you sons of bitches. You're the only ones with guts enough to *really* care about the future, who *really* notice what machines do to us, what wars do to us, what cities do to us, what tremendous misunderstandings, mistakes, accidents, and catastrophes do to us. You're the only ones zany enough to agonize over time and distances without limit, over mysteries that will never die, over the fact that we are right now determining whether the space voyage for the next billion years or so is going to be Heaven or Hell.

The drunken hero of KURT VONNEGUT's God
Bless You, Mr. Rosewater, *who blunders into a
convention of science fiction writers*

You can be a little ungrammatical if you come from the right part of the country.

ROBERT FROST

The crown of literature is poetry. It is its end and aim. It is the sublimest activity of the human mind. It is the achievement of beauty and delicacy. The writer of prose can only step aside when the poet passes.

W. SOMERSET MAUGHAM

Everybody has their own idea of what's a poet. Robert
Frost, President Johnson, T. S. Eliot, Rudolf Valentino—
they're all poets. I like to think of myself as the one who
carries the light bulb.

BOB DYLAN

You don't have to suffer to be a poet. Adolescence is
enough suffering for anyone.

JOHN CIARDI

When power leads man to arrogance, poetry reminds
him of his limitations. When power narrows the area of
man's concern, poetry reminds him of the richness and
diversity of his existence. When power corrupts, poetry
cleanses.

PRESIDENT JOHN KENNEDY, *October 26,
1963 at the dedication of the Robert Frost Library, Amherst College*

Poets aren't very useful.
Because they aren't consumeful or very produceful.

OGDEN NASH

Like a piece of ice on a hot stove the poem must ride on
its own melting.

ROBERT FROST

Publishing a volume of verse is like dropping a rose-petal
down the Grand Canyon and waiting for the echo.

DON MARQUIS

I've had it with these cheap sons of bitches who claim they love poetry but never buy a book.

KENNETH REXROTH

Modesty is a virtue not often found among poets, for almost every one of them thinks himself the greatest in the world.

MIGUEL DE CERVANTES

Respect the children of the poor—from them come most poets.

MENDELE MOCHER SFORIM

It's silly to suggest the writing of poetry as something ethereal, a sort of soul-crashing emotional experience that wrings you. I have no fancy ideas about poetry. It doesn't come to you on the wings of a dove. It's something you work hard at.

LOUISE BOGAN

Great poetry is always written by somebody straining to go beyond what he can do.

STEPHEN SPENDER

I went for years not finishing anything. Because, of course, when you finish something you can be judged. . . . I had poems which were re-written so many times I suspect it was just a way of avoiding sending them out.

ERICA JONG

If I feel physically as if the top of my head were taken off, I know that is poetry.

EMILY DICKINSON

I could no more define poetry than a terrier can define a rat.

A. E. HOUSMAN

A true sonnet goes eight lines and then takes a turn for the better or worse and goes six or eight lines more.

ROBERT FROST

Were poets to be suppressed, my friends, with no history, no ancient lays, save that each had a father, nothing of any man would be heard hereafter.

GIOLLA BRIGHDE MHAC CON MIDH
(circa 1259)

A good writer is not, per se, a good book critic. No more than a good drunk is automatically a good bartender.

JIM BISHOP

I regard reviews as a kind of infant's disease to which newborn books are subject.

GEORG CHRISTOPH   LICHTENBERG

A unanimous chorus of approval is not an assurance of survival; authors who please everyone at once are quickly exhausted.

ANDRÉ GIDE

It is advantageous to an author that his book should be attacked as well as praised. Fame is a shuttlecock. If it be struck at only one end of the room, it will soon fall to the ground. To keep it up, it must be struck at both ends.

SAMUEL JOHNSON

Nature fits all her children with something to do;
He who would write and can't write, can surely review.

JAMES RUSSELL LOWELL

It is as hard to find a neutral critic as it is a neutral country in time of war. I suppose if a critic were neutral, he wouldn't trouble to write anything.

KATHERINE ANNE PORTER

I am sitting in the smallest room in my house. I have your review in front of me. Soon it will be behind me.

German composer MAX REGER

A person who publishes a book willfully appears before the populace with his pants down. . . . If it is a good book nothing can hurt him. If it is a bad book, nothing can help him.

EDNA ST. VINCENT MILLAY

When a man publishes a book, there are so many stupid things said that he declares he'll never do it again. The praise is almost always worse than the criticism.

SHERWOOD ANDERSON

Confronted by an absolutely infuriating review it is sometimes helpful for the victim to do a little personal research on the critic. Is there any truth to the rumor that he had no formal education beyond the age of eleven? In any event, is he able to construct a simple English sentence? Do his participles dangle? When moved to lyricism does he write "I had a fun time"? Was he ever arrested for burglary? I don't know that you will prove anything this way, but it is perfectly harmless and quite soothing.

JEAN KERR

Listen carefully to first criticisms of your work. Note just what it is about your work that the critics don't like—then cultivate it. That's the part of your work that's individual and worth keeping.

JEAN COCTEAU

The relation of the agent to the publisher is the same as that of the knife to the throat.

ANONYMOUS

Let every eye negotiate for itself, and trust no agent.

WILLIAM SHAKESPEARE

The new race of academic reviewers may be cleverer, more conscientious, fairer than those who went before and they may take their job more seriously, but they are a complete disaster from everyone's point of view— publisher, book buyer, writer—because practically no one reads them. It is not just that they assume a higher dedication and a higher level of seriousness than exists among most intelligent, educated novel readers. They are quite simply too dull.

AUBERON WAUGH

Dick was a superb salesman, and the very fact that he hadn't read the books made him able to sell them that much better. Some of the best Hollywood agents, for instance, are the same. They can sell movie rights for much more when they haven't read a book than if they have.

BENNETT CERF

Calvin Trillin once proposed that "the advance for a book should be at least as much as the cost of the lunch at which it was discussed." When he asked an editor what he thought of this formula, he was told that it was "unrealistic."

WILLARD ESPY

No passion in the world is equal to the passion to alter someone else's draft.

H. G. WELLS

The editorial job has become, unlike the ancient age when one judged what one read, a job of making judgements on outlines, ideas, reputations, previous books, scenarios, treatments, talk and promises.

SAM VAUGHAN

An editor should tell the author his writing is better than it is. Not a lot better, a little better.

T. S. ELIOT

Don't get involved, or show paternal anxiety, unless you intend publishing the author's work.

WILLIAM TARG

My relationship with every writer who was dear to us had constantly to be redefined. What is true of friendship is true of editing; the understanding must be continually refreshed. . . . I have tried to remember that it was my job to help when the author needed it, to reassure him, to call out of him his best, but always to bear in mind that the final decision was his.

EDWARD WEEKS

Editors are extremely fallible people, all of them. Don't put too much trust in them.

MAXWELL PERKINS

Great editors do not discover nor produce great authors; great authors create and produce great publishers.

JOHN FARRAR

Never buy an editor or publisher a lunch or a drink until he has bought an article, story or book from you. This rule is absolute and may be broken only at your peril.

JOHN CREASEY

Editors at work

The stories of childhood leave an indelible impression, and their author always has a niche in the temple of memory from which the image is never cast out to be thrown on the rubbish heap of things that are outgrown and outlived.

HOWARD PYLE

You know how it is in the kid's book world: It's just bunny eat bunny.

ANONYMOUS

Editors have responsible jobs, and they should be highly paid; unfortunately, in most cases, they get miserable salaries and capable men do not remain in such jobs. Editors are the immemorial adversaries of writers, because most editors are editors because they wanted to be writers and failed, and they instinctively hate those who wanted to be writers and succeeded.

JACK WOODFORD

An acquiring editor is someone who enjoys making love to strangers.

TOM CONGDON

The very last time we were with Faulkner was at "21" in 1962. It was then that he talked to me about Albert Erskine, who became his editor after Saxe Commins died. Faulkner said, "You know, I think Albert is the best book editor I know." I said, "Golly, Bill, coming from William Faulkner that's quite an encomium. Have you told Albert?" He paused for a minute, then said, "No, I haven't, Bennett. When I've got a horse that's running good, I don't stop him to give him some sugar."

BENNETT CERF

Acquiring editors acquire.
Remark made by an anonymous editor when told of two prominent editors at one house who had four and five wives respectively

Everyone needs an editor.
TIM FOOTE *commenting in* Time *magazine upon the fact that Hitler's original title for* Mein Kampf *was* Four-and-a-Half Years of Struggle against Lies, Stupidity, and Cowardice

The one thing I have learned about editing over the years is that you have to edit and publish out of your own tastes, enthusiasms, and concerns, and not out of notions or guesswork about what other people might like to read.

NORMAN COUSINS

The greatest obstacle to good book publishing is the editorial board. One seasoned editor's judgement is of greater value than a committee of six.

WILLIAM TARG

A competent editor is a publisher in microcosm, able to initiate and follow a project all the way through.

MARC JAFFE

Gone today, here tomorrow.
ALFRED KNOPF *on book returns*

Publishers are demons, there's no doubt about it.
WILLIAM JAMES

There are men that will make you books and turn 'em loose into the world with as much dispatch as they would do a dish of fritters.
MIGUEL DE CERVANTES

People feel no obligation to buy books. It isn't their fault. Art seems cheap to them, because almost always it is cheap. . . . People stick any kind of stuff together between covers and throw it at them.
SHERWOOD ANDERSON

Until the manuscript is delivered, power is shared. When the manuscript enters the publishing process, power shifts to the publisher. It is the publisher who decides how the book is presented to the public.
TED SOLOTAROFF

Publishers will tell you, with their tongue in their cheek, that every manuscript which reaches their office is faithfully read, but they are not to be believed. At least fifteen out of twenty manuscripts can be summarily rejected, usually with safety. There may be a masterpiece among them, but it is a thousand to one against.
MICHAEL JOSEPH

Another illusion, seldom entertained by competent authors, is that the publisher's readers and others are waiting to plagiarize their work. I think it may be said that the more worthless the manuscript, the greater the fear of plagiarism.

SIR STANLEY UNWIN

Publishing is a very mysterious business. It is hard to predict what kind of sale or reception a book will have, and advertising seems to do very little good.

THOMAS WOLFE *in a letter to his mother*

A small press is an attitude, a kind of anti-commerciality. The dollars come second, the talent and the quality of the writing come first. If the presses wanted to make money, they'd be out there selling cookbooks.

BILL HENDERSON

A small publisher really should, if he can, stay away from fiction.

ALAN SWALLOW

To write books is easy, it requires only pen and ink and the ever-patient paper. To print books is a little more difficult, because genius so often rejoices in illegible handwriting. To read books is more difficult still, because of the tendency to go to sleep. But the most difficult task of all that a mortal man can embark on is to sell a book.

from a poem by FELIX DAHN *paraphrased by*
SIR STANLEY UNWIN

My co-authors call me up and get hysterical if the book isn't in Brentano's. I say, "tough luck." If I have an idea for a new display or promotion, I'll send it to the publisher. It's no good sitting back and saying the publisher stinks.

SAMM SINCLAIR BAKER

Most authors are born to be failures, and the publisher knows it. He makes his living out of the few successes, and if he is indulgent with less successful writers, it is not only because there is always the possibility that today's failure may become tomorrow's best-seller. Unless he has a genuine sympathy with the author's problems, no one can hope to make an enduring success of publishing.

MICHAEL JOSEPH

. . . of making many books there is no end.

ECCLESIASTES 12:12

THE WRITER'S QUOTATION BOOK
was typeset by Bob McCoy in Sabon, a typeface designed by
Jan Tschichold. Ann Schroeder designed the book and selected
the illustrations. The book was printed on Glatfelter's Writer's
Offset by Ray Freiman and Co., Stamford, Connecticut.
Production was coordinated by The Word Guild,
Cambridge, Massachusetts.

This book was produced for the publisher,
by Ray Freiman & Company
Stamford, Connecticut 06903